Get Customers Online

~

Get Customers Online

Marketing that Grows Sales, Website Traffic, and Business

ERIC CARLIN

Copyright © 2017 Eric Carlin
All rights reserved. No part of this publication may be reproduced or transmitted in any form or by any means without prior written permission from the copyright owner.

Printed in the United States of America

First Printing, 2017

ISBN-13: 978-0692893340
ISBN-10: 0692893342

For more information on this publication, contact Eric Carlin via www.ad-bliss.com/contact

Dedicated to the go-getters who want to create synergy between business and marketing online.

~

Table of Contents

Chapter 1: Search Marketing..................................10

    Intercept Customers in Search Engines.....11

    Win More Business with Messaging..........13

    Making the Most of Search Marketing......16

    Action Checklist..20

Chapter 2: Online Advertising...............................21

    Establishing an Irresistible Brand...............22

    Becoming Undeniably Relevant..................24

    Advertising to Previous Website Visitors………………………………….....26

    Action Checklist..28

Chapter 3: Retargeting Ads....................................29

    Positioning Your Brand to Customers Online...30

    Generating Returning Customers...............32

    Converting Website Visitors into Leads...34

    Action Checklist..37

Chapter 4: Social Media Marketing.......................38

    Maximizing Brand Exposure.......................39

    Growing from Voice-of-the-Customer.......41

- Social Media Advertising..........................44
- Action Checklist...48

Chapter 5: Email Marketing..................................49
- Email Content that Adds Value...............50
- Marketing Your Email Newsletter..........53
- Encouraging Customer Opt-in................56
- Action Checklist...59

Chapter 6: Website Content..................................60
- Enhancing Visibility of Online Content..61
- Driving Sales with Web Experiences......62
- Ensuring Customer-centricity in Content..64
- Action Checklist...67

Chapter 7: Digital Analytics..................................68
- URL Tracking..69
- Tag Management.......................................71
- Convert More Website Visitors into Customers..73
- Action Checklist...76

Introduction

You want to gain more visibility of your website and brand online, but you haven't determined how that can grow your business. As a small business, startup, or novice marketer, I hope this book will empower you to begin or expand your online marketing efforts.

Get Customers Online aims to create synergy between business and marketing online for companies in any industry. Learn about 21 actionable growth opportunities to increase:

- sales
- leads
- website traffic
- brand awareness

You will receive guidance for execution, along with insights for maintenance and measurement. With *Get Customers Online*, you will have knowledge to transform online visibility into business results which include:

- gaining new and returning customers online
- increasing visibility of your online content for awareness of products, services, and brand
- differentiating your brand from the competition to win more business online
- measuring and adjusting to drive more results from your efforts

Search Marketing

Intercept Customers in Search Engines

Successful search marketing begins by using search advertisements and your website to target relevant words and phrases being searched by customers. Those words and phrases that you target are also known as keywords. When your website appears in search results, it is because your keywords were relevant to the search terms chosen by customers. This is most helpful for businesses when they need to attract customers who are searching for products, services, or simply browsing the web for the hottest, new commodity.

Search marketing is your opportunity to reach customers when they are seeking what you offer. If your keywords and site content match the customers' intent, you can increase the odds that search engines will view your site as meaningful and include it in search results.

However, your site and advertisements are less likely to appear in search results if you do not target keywords relevant to what customers are seeking. This is because you haven't shown that your website can meet the customers' needs.

> "Your site and advertisements are less likely to appear in search results if you do not target keywords relevant to what customers are seeking."

Before you start creating ads and site content that offer a solution for customers, you must find out what they are searching. Start your research by talking to a group of your ideal customers so you can understand their intent and search terms when searching the internet for a product or website like yours.

It is the customers' intent that will connect the dots for you when you begin researching valuable keywords to target. No matter how broad or how niche your intended audience is, your customers will browse the internet much different than audiences in other target markets. Because they have unique browsing behavior, your success at search marketing will depend on how well your website taps into your customers' intent.

Once you have spoken with a group of customers and gained some meaningful insights, you can begin seeking out keywords that will deliver powerful results. Many keyword research tools are available for free online. The advantage of these tools is that they help you identify the most valuable keywords being searched.

At a high level, a valuable keyword has a combination of:

- high search volume
- low to medium competition
- relevancy to the webpage appearing in search results

Keep in mind that search marketing is a continuing

effort. Your presence in search engines should evolve with your business so you're always reflecting the current offerings of your business. As you expand your website and search advertisements with new offerings, your keyword research and implementation processes will begin again. With the experience that you gain each time, the process will become easier.

Measure the opportunity available to intercept customers within results by identifying the average position where you rank for various keywords. Some online tools will also tell you the average position where your competitors land when they appear for a keyword.

When you find that detailed information, take advantage by analyzing your competitors' website content and search advertisements. This should help you understand how they are writing content to present relevancy between the same customer needs and search terms. With this, you will gain insights about how to enhance your keyword targeting and win more business in search engines.

Win More Business with Messaging

Win more business with a differentiated message that sets you apart from the competition. After implementing keywords across your website, you will need to maximize your odds of getting clicks from the search results where you appear. After all, the point of search marketing is to gain more website traffic and the business that comes from it.

All customers will need a motive for clicking through to your website. That motive is the content you present to them in search results. Those results offer two outlets for you to communicate the unique value of your business.

In search advertisements, they are known as headlines and descriptions. In organic search results, they are known as page descriptions and title tags. Using those outlets successfully requires concise messages that differentiate you from others in the results so customers click through.

> "All customers will need a motive for clicking through to your website. That motive is the content you present to them in search results."

If you choose not to add your own content into your website's page descriptions and title tags, search engines will automatically fill in those blank spaces with other content from your website. While automation like that makes the process easier, you lose the opportunity to generate clicks with customer-focused content that is infused with your brand's personality.

When writing the messages for your search marketing, speak to the problem that your products or services solve. Those solutions should connect with the customers' intent that you learn directly from them. Articulate your solutions in a way that differentiates your brand from others who are offering comparable solutions.

As noted earlier, search marketing is a continuing effort. The maintenance of your search marketing messages should revolve around the evolution of your business and the industry. As the value proposition of your products or services evolves, so should the messages you present to customers in search engines. And, as your industry evolves, your customers' desires and expectations will reflect those changes. Therefore, you not only need to update your messages as your business shifts, but also as the industry shifts.

"As the value proposition of your products or services evolves, so should the messages you present to customers in search engines."

Measure the success of your messaging in search engines with metrics such as impressions, clicks, and click-through rate.

- Impressions are the amount of times that your website appeared in search results
- Clicks are the amount of times that customers were directed from a search result to your website
- Click-through rate is the percentage of impressions that generated clicks

These metrics indicate the rate at which customers are seeing your search engine messages and becoming intrigued enough to click to your website.

As you begin analyzing keyword searches to find which brought you the most website traffic, group together the keywords that resulted in the highest and lowest click-through rates.

If you have reason to believe that your click-through rates could be higher, you will want to analyze the differences between your high-performing and low-performing webpages. You may find discrepancies in your keyword targeting or the content in your search marketing messages.

First, review the keywords that your low-performing webpages are targeting and ask yourself how relevant those keywords are to that webpage. If you can reasonably defend their relevancy, move on to what else may be causing your low click-through rate. As I've discussed already, search marketing is a competitive landscape, which means you must differentiate yourself.

Analyze the search marketing messages of your high-performing webpages in comparison to content you wrote for the low-performing webpages. You may find some common traits among the webpages with higher click-through rates and afterwards, you may notice that those common traits are missing from the webpages with the low click-through rates.

Making the Most of Search Marketing

Search marketing is broken down into paid search and organic search. Paid search refers to targeted advertisements that appear in search results. The advantage to paid search is that you can target any keywords that are relevant to your webpage and advertisement. The advanced targeting options of paid search make it much easier to win business in the competitive landscape of search results. This especially holds true when your website is struggling to organically appear on the first page of search results.

Organic search refers to a website appearing in search results at no cost due to the relevancy between a customer's search term and content on a website. The advantage of organic search is that when your website does appear, it's probably very relevant to a customer's search term and therefore worthy of clicks at no cost.

For many businesses, organic search has become a sustainable and profitable source of website traffic. However, the reality is that you will not always appear above or anywhere near your competition with organic search alone. That is when paid search can become worth the cost.

Assess which keyword searches you have targeted through organic search but did not achieve. Before you give up hope to appear organically for those keywords, you may need to revisit your webpages to ensure the content there is relevant.

If you have done what you can to ensure your webpages achieve a high position in organic search results, and your competition is crowding the results for the keywords you are targeting, it may be time to enlist paid search.

First, identify your objective for targeting those keyword searches and what you could gain by receiving clicks to your website from those searches. The traffic you gain could:

- generate leads
- increase online sales
- build awareness of your brand, product, or service

If you estimate a profitable return by appearing in a competitive search result, begin targeting your paid search advertisements at those search terms. That can assist you in intercepting customers before others by giving you a prominent placement in the results.

Optimize your search marketing performance by measuring and realigning on a common, scheduled basis.

Run organic search marketing reports monthly and give attention to any significant changes such as a decrease in your site's average positon in search results. Run paid search marketing reports weekly. If you notice in a paid search report that you are targeting keyword searches where you already appear in organic search results, you can reduce costs by pausing those paid advertisements from appearing.

"Optimize your search marketing performance by measuring and realigning on a common, scheduled basis."

As you dedicate time to reviewing your search advertisements, realign your budgets, keywords, and targeting so they provide a profitable return on your ad spend. This time is critical because you can find opportunities to cut unnecessary costs and generate more traffic. Keep an eye out for under-performing keywords, pause your ads from appearing when those are searched, then re-allocate that money to more valuable keyword searches so you increase clicks without increasing your budget.

Action Checklist

1. Identify which products or services on your website you want to promote.

2. Talk with customers from your target audience to understand their intent and search terms when searching the internet for a product or website like yours.

3. Find a free online tool to conduct keyword research using the insights you gather from customers.

4. Create site content and search advertisements that are extremely relevant to the keywords and audiences that you are targeting.

5. Write search marketing messages that connect the intent of your customers with the solutions that your brand offers.

6. Manage a profitable search marketing portfolio with a savvy mix of organic search results and paid search advertisements.

Online Advertising

Establishing an Irresistible Brand

Establish an irresistible brand in the minds of customers. By advertising with video or images online, you can communicate your brand's messaging and promote your solutions. This is your opportunity to develop ad concepts and content that captivates customers and differentiates you from competitors in the market.

Creating ads that appeal to your audience will require research. Try to connect with a group of your ideal customers and gather their input on what differentiates your brand from others. Choose questions that will provide actionable insights for your ad. You should be able identify why customers choose your products or services instead of the competition.

"Develop ad concepts and content that captivates customers and differentiates you from competitors in the market."

Dig beyond vague feedback that simply tells you that your company is "better." There isn't anything actionable about being better. Perhaps your company is the only industry player that offers a specific promotion, product feature, or service.

Ensure that the research you conducted with your customers is used in your ads. Your customers will provide insights that are more powerful than a generic ad concept that speaks to no one other than its creator. Your online ads should resonate with viewers by connecting the customers' values to your brand's mission.

Your messages can change minds and establish a foundation for customers to trust your brand to solve their everyday problems. Because of this, management of your digital presence is critical to long-term success.

As your brand or industry evolves, the ad concepts and messages that you present must evolve as well. If you stay well-informed on the evolving needs of customers and act in a timely manner, your advertising performance will reflect your willingness to adapt.

The key performance indicators for online advertisements vary based on your objective. If your intention for ads is to begin positioning your brand within the minds of customers, your key performance indicators could revolve around:

- the amount of impressions your ad gathers
- increases in brand-related searches
- the quality of traffic brought to your website

Metrics such as those will help you scale to more meaningful volumes of impressions over time as you identify how well those ad campaigns helped you achieve your business objectives.

When analyzing the quality of website traffic that

your ads generate, measure the actions customers take on your website such as online purchases, the amount of customers who navigated to a sales-related page, and the value of returning visitors. Learning about the quality of your website traffic will signal if you need to refine the audiences being targeted with your ads.

Becoming Undeniably Relevant

Become undeniably relevant in your market by positioning your brand in the center of conversations online. One critical advantage of online advertising is the ease of targeting your ads at all the right websites and mobile apps. Some options to pinpoint where your ads appear include:

- website URL or mobile app
- topics of site content
- keywords in site content

Identify which websites and apps are the hubs for trending topics in your industry, plus any topics of content published by other online sources. Targeting your ads at such websites will allow your brand to disrupt the norm with differentiated messages that drive site traffic.

When your ads entice customers to click-through to your website, the customers are directed to your landing page. Right away, your landing page should present content that follows up on the ad's message. This is your opportunity to build a conversation that relates to your solutions and your brand.

If your landing page content is going to keep visitors engaged, it needs to add value to what they saw in the ad. The advantage of a landing page is that it provides you with control of the conversation and you can steer potential customers towards your own solutions.

> "Right away, your landing page should present content that follows up on the ad's message."

Not only does a successful landing page provide valuable content, it also generates leads or sales. The content should go a step beyond just the significance of your brand. Show visitors that your solutions are a match for their needs. Invite them to fill out a short contact form on the landing page or lead them to an e-commerce section of your website to make a purchase.

When analyzing the success of these ad campaigns, measure the ad impressions, the click-through rate, and the number of visitors that took an action on your landing page such as making a purchase. It will take a lot of visibility for your ad impressions to make a strong impact on sales or lead generation. But as you go, the amount of ad impressions you purchase can scale as your sales or leads grow. The increased exposure could lead to higher sales which, in turn, can enable you to finance larger campaigns.

Analyze which websites and apps are responsible for

your highest rate of click-throughs so you identify where your target market resides online. From there, you can stop paying for ads on sites that contribute to significantly fewer customer actions on your site. To become more relevant in your industry, spend your ad dollars on websites and apps where customers are connecting with your brand's message.

Advertising to Previous Website Visitors

Generate returning website customers and visitors with retargeting. Just like in a brick-and-mortar store, many customers will visit your website just to browse, then leave without initiating a transaction or a request for information. But unlike a brick-and-mortar store, you can easily communicate with those lost website visitors again.

The tactic is called retargeting. With retargeting, you can reach customers that recently visited your website and achieve multiple objectives.

- Enhance awareness of your brand, products, or services
- Generate returning customers for online sales
- Convert previous website visitors into leads

This form of online advertising should be a strategic addition to your marketing plan. For it to be successful, it must be an extension to other marketing initiatives and create an extra touchpoint between you and your customers.

For example, many businesses rely on social media for building awareness of their brand. After driving social media followers to their website, a business could retarget those same visitors across other social media apps.

Those ads could be related to webpages the social media followers showed an interest in like a product or service. This leaves no limits to the brand's exposure while also keeping the customers interested in the brand's offerings.

"With retargeting, you can reach customers that recently visited your website."

When you have an objective to build more awareness of your business, retargeting can be a powerful piece of that strategy because your audience has already shown an interest in your business. The awareness you create could be focused on your offerings or simply around the brand messaging that you believe can propel your business forward in the market. Hopefully that interest will cause them to be more receptive to your messages.

Other objectives for retargeting include advertising to customers who did or did not take a specific action on a website. Whether a website's purpose is for e-commerce or an extension of your brand, you can make retargeting ads a profitable tactic by enticing customers to return to your website for a newly-released product or learn more about what you sell.

Action Checklist

1. Speak with customers to identify what differentiates your brand from others in the industry.

2. Captivate customers with messages that reflect why your ideal customers buy from your brand.

3. Target your advertisements at industry websites and mobile apps that are the hubs for trending topics.

4. Use your landing pages as a branded environment to engage customers with conversation about your products and services.

5. Extend your marketing initiatives by retargeting previous website visitors who are likely to be receptive to your message.

Retargeting Ads

Positioning Your Brand to Customers Online

The days of needing a spray-n-pray approach to advertising are long gone. With online advertising, you have multiple options for narrowly targeting any audience with your ads. An effective way to target your ads is to reach previous website visitors, also called retargeting.

Retargeting allows you to advertise your brand to customers who previously showed interest in your offerings and could therefore be receptive to your messages. Based on your objectives, these ads can be targeted at anyone who previously visited your website, viewers of a specific webpage such as a product, or customers with a previous transaction on your site.

> "Advertise your brand to customers who previously showed interest in your offerings and could therefore be receptive to your messaging."

Couple your brand's messaging with retargeting ads to build upon perceptions that visitors gained while they were on your company's site. Doing so could help you stay relevant in the market among an audience that is possibly receptive to learning more.

Retargeting can also help you achieve an objective that is tied to your products or services. You may choose to advertise your newest product line to visitors, for example. Whether you execute online sales or not, following up with visitors by using retargeting can keep your products at the top of your customers' minds while they browse the web, increasing your odds of a sale.

Like product sales, these targeted ad campaigns can also assist professional services companies with reaching visitors who navigated to a webpage related to services. With such targeting, your brand can articulate the value proposition of those services and simultaneously entice customers to visit again for more valuable information that will move them along in their journey.

Impressions are a critical metric for retargeting ads when your priority is to generate awareness of your brand, product, or service. You may not see short-term gains from this tactic so you will need to prepare a budget, measurement, and optimization plan to suit a long-term campaign.

You will often pay per thousand impressions of your ad which means that you won't pay when customers click through to your website. Due to that advantage, these campaigns can be cheaper than paying per click if a high percentage of viewers click through. To achieve that, ensure that your ad:

- targets visitors with content that is relevant to what they viewed on your site
- connects customer needs to your solutions
- has a captivating design

When you measure the effectiveness of these ad campaigns, analyze which variations of your ads entice a higher percentage of viewers to click through to your website. By reviewing the percentage of ad impressions that resulted in a click, you can compare various ad messages, designs, and targeting methods to identify your most valuable combinations and optimize the return on your ad spend.

By knowing the return on your ad spend, you can always justify your next move such as reaching more viewers of your ads with a higher budget.

Generating Returning Customers

Retargeting ads that are tailored based on your customers' purchasing history can assist e-commerce websites in generating returning customers. With a combination of web analytics and retargeting, an e-commerce business can segment its previous customers based on their interactions with your website, then target various customer segments with unique, tailored advertisements. That means segments of customers can see ads that are related to their recent activity and receive relevant incentives to return.

If you sell clothes from a popular brand and begin carrying their new products for the upcoming season, you can retarget customers who previously bought items from that brand on your e-commerce website. Ads like that would be tailored based on the customers' purchasing history and therefore have greater potential for success.

"Target various customer segments with unique, tailored advertisements."

To begin defining segments of customers that will receive advertisements, it's critical that you identify the interval of time between your customers' initial purchase and their return to purchase again.

For example, if many of your first-time customers return within 30 days to make a second purchase, you can retarget customers that did not return within 30 days and offer a discount on your ad's landing page to encourage a purchase. Whether it's a discount offer or something more relevant to your business, the concept of retargeting is that you can communicate with those customers who did not return and entice them to complete another transaction. However, these ads aren't restricted to customers who haven't returned within a specified amount of time.

Due to the flexibility provided by web analytics tools, you could also create a segment of customers who have made multiple purchases within a relatively short amount of time. By targeting a specific audience that has shown loyalty and potential to buy more, you can avoid spending your marketing budget on customers who are unlikely to purchase.

Additionally, your existing customers may benefit from seeing advertisements that introduce your newest products. With the flexibility to define the best audience for each ad, you can drive profitable returns from advertisements of your newest offerings.

The most practical way to bid on these sales-oriented ads is to pay per click. This form of bidding means that you will only pay for customers who showed enough interest in your product to follow the ad to your website. When paying per click on your ad, your costs can increase quickly so you must first identify how much you are willing to spend, then monitor the online sales that you generate to determine the return on your ad spend.

Calculating your return on ad spend will signal a successful or failing combination of your ad costs and ability of your website to convert traffic into customers. You can calculate your return on ad spend by dividing the revenue from your ads by the cost of your ads. With this metric, you can determine the revenue you made for every dollar spent on your retargeting campaigns.

Converting Website Visitors into Leads

Lead generation occurs across a variety of touchpoints, and retargeting ads are one touchpoint that can be beneficial for companies that want to generate leads online. The advantage of adding retargeting to your lead generation strategy is that you can tailor ads and their landing pages to meet the needs that are unique to each segment of customers. With the flexibility to retarget segments of viewers of your service or product, you can influence their return with a tailored message and entice them to request more information.

To take advantage of this targeted advertising, craft your ad messages to build upon webpage content that your audience read when they visited your webpage. This will sustain the perception that you already presented. As you develop the ad content, draw connections between your customers' needs and your offerings while remaining unique in comparison to competitors. Due to the connection that you can create with those messages, your ads will be more likely to generate website traffic.

> "Craft your ad messages to build upon webpage content that your audience read when they visited your webpage."

After creating ads designed to improve perceptions of your offerings, you may want to create separate landing pages for each offering. The webpages that viewers will land on after clicking your ads are your opportunity to convert them into a lead. Simply leading those customers to the same webpage that they visited before will not help; they didn't convert there initially and are unlikely to change their mind on a second viewing. By creating a webpage with content that builds upon what these customers already know about your offerings, you can encourage consideration rather than simply satisfy their research for a solution.

Measurement of your advertisements and their landing pages will be critical to success in lead generation. One occurrence that you may experience is your ads producing a low volume of website traffic.

In these situations, keep in mind that each segment of customers viewed an offering specific to their interests when they originally visited your website. Therefore, you should test variations of messages on your ad campaigns to determine which is most relevant to each segment of customers. You may find a combination of ad content that better entices traffic to click through to your website.

If you experience a low percentage of web traffic converting into leads from your landing pages, you should test multiple variations of webpage content until you find a combination of information and calls to action that entice more customers to convert.

Action Checklist

1. Define the scope of your audiences that will be served retargeting ads.

2. Segment previous customers based on their interactions with your website, then target each customer segment with tailored advertisements.

3. Couple your brand's messaging with retargeting ads to build upon perceptions that visitors gained while they were on your company's website.

4. Craft your messages to build upon what your audience read when they previously visited your webpage.

5. Lead traffic to landing pages that encourage consideration of your offerings rather than simply satisfying the customers' research for a solution.

6. Generate returning customers with retargeting ads that are tailored based on your customers' purchasing history.

Social Media Marketing

Maximizing Brand Exposure

Maximize the reach of your brand, products, and services by publishing marketing content across multiple networks. The social media landscape continues to grow, offering new content formats for brands and individuals to use. This means, the latest news about your company doesn't have to be confined to only a few outlets. Marketing content can be massaged for multiple formats and then delivered to more customers.

The various content formats across social media platforms can be used strategically to increase exposure to your marketing messages. Whether your company is just beginning social media marketing or is ready to expand its presence across more platforms, it's critical that you identify the platforms where your audience is most receptive to content from your industry. Do some research and identify competitors with a prominent social media presence to learn which platforms generate the most interactions such as comments, likes, shares, etc.

"It's critical that you identify the platforms where your audience is most receptive to content from your industry."

Aside from understanding customer behavior in your industry, the research should also uncover which content formats other industry players are using to publish marketing messages. This competitive view of how content is published will help you to strategically choose formats for your various content themes on social media. Align the research you conduct with a goal of choosing a manageable number of platforms and content formats to maximize the exposure of your marketing messages.

Consider the objectives that your marketing content should achieve through those content formats such as encouraging interactions with your brand or leading customers to your website. Your content will perform best with content formats that compliment it.

A company whose objective is to market their brand lifestyle will see more customer interaction with their posts if they use images or video rather than text. Similarly, an event may be better suited for a live video format if you want to interact with customers who could not attend the event. Defining content objectives such as these will help you publish content strategically with various formats across social media platforms.

> "Publish content strategically with various formats across social media platforms."

After you finalize your choices of social media platforms and content formats, you must identify their primary and secondary uses. Keep in mind that your objective is to maximize the reach of your marketing messages by using the same content across multiple platforms. That is accomplished by first documenting which content formats you will use on each platform such as:

- live video
- disappearing video
- photos

Following that, you must define which content formats will be the primary source for some content themes. Perhaps you choose live video as your content format for events so you can interact with customers who are not participating in the actual event.

Once you have defined which content formats will be the primary sources for each content theme, you should identify a secondary platform and format for each theme.

Following the most recent example of using live video for events, you may choose to use photos from the event on a separate platform so you extend your reach to more viewers. Photos can provide a glimpse of the event action and by also including a caption, you can provide meaningful snippets of event details to customers who are not watching your live video.

Growing from Voice-of-the-Customer

Social media offers a direct line between brands and their customers, and the interactions that occur can be valuable for both parties. Customers want better experiences from brands and brands must provide it if they want to continue growing. Designate time in your schedule to interact with customers through social media and uncover opportunities for growth.

The value of such engagement with customers will depend on the clear objectives you set for enhancing their experiences. Engage customers with the goal of gaining specific feedback about anything critical to their experiences such as product information, shipping concerns, or experiences with your website.

> "Designate time in your schedule to interact with customers through social media and uncover opportunities for growth."

While managing your social media platforms, you should take note of which platforms and content formats are generating the most interactions between your brand and customers. By analyzing that history between your brand and customers, you can identify which combination of platforms and content formats will generate the most responses from your social media followers when you ask them for it.

For example, you may notice that your social media polls often drive a large volume of responses, so you then choose a poll to identify which enhancements in your product lines would be most enticing to your customers.

Successfully interacting with customers through social media requires monitoring of all platforms where your brand has a presence. By monitoring multiple platforms from one online tool that aggregates interactions with your brand, you can quickly respond to more customers so that you:

- close sales
- avoid a backlog of feedback and questions
- learn about enhancements that your customers want for better experiences

Keep in mind that customer feedback may not always come directly to your profiles or inboxes. Often you may gather valuable insights from your customers responding to others in your comments or using hashtags that are relevant to your industry.

While customers often point out profitable opportunities for business growth, it's critical that you have a plan for analyzing the potential behind their requests. Simply making a judgement call about the potential value in each request could hold you back from enhancing your customers' experiences and generating additional revenue.

When any project crosses your desk, you will need to assess the risks and consider whether it's aligned with your company's objectives. In addition to analyzing the costs, revenue and profit potential, your assessments should also consider whether the project would receive support from a large segment of your customers and whether there are risks due to the nature of your market.

If you plan to compare the potential outcomes of

multiple projects, you will need to use a grading scale that scores each project based on their risks and value. For example, if your assessment has 10 data points, you could grade the risk or value of each data point with a score of 1 to 10. Once you combine those scores from each data point, you would receive a final score out of one hundred. Afterwards, you could review the projects with the highest scores to identify which will meet your business objectives.

Social Media Advertising

Reach new customers with ads that help your business achieve its objectives such as increasing online sales or building awareness of your brand. By advertising on social media, your ads can be targeted to new customers whose demographics and interests resemble those of your existing customers.

The criteria you choose will cause your ad to target users whose profile information is a match. For example, if your business sells jewelry online and your most valuable customers are females in the age range of 18-25, you can pay to serve ads only to that audience. This can be a profitable tactic for achieving your business objectives because your investment goes towards reaching highly-relevant customers.

To successfully target your ads based on the demographics and interests of your existing customers, you should define the details of your target audience. A target audience is a group that your advertisements will reach. Following the previous example, this could be females in the age range of 18-25 who often purchase jewelry from online retailers. Simple details like these can be useful for finding new customers online that match the interests and demographics of your existing customers.

> "Your ads can be targeted to new customers whose demographics and interests resemble those of your existing customers."

The targeting criteria that will help grow each business can vary, but some examples to get you started include:

- Interests
- Geographic location
- Occupation
- Age
- Gender

Once you've targeted a segment of customers, your social media ads can be served to people within that audience who are likely to take a specific action. This goes beyond writing ad content that calls upon customers to visit your website.

By advertising on social media, your ads can be served to the right customers at the right time so they take the actions you desire such as making a purchase on your website. This can help you achieve your business objectives and see a return on your ad spend because you can anticipate that customers will interact with your ads in a specific manner.

If an online jewelry retailer wanted to increase online sales, ads could be served to customers who are most likely to purchase. However, if that same retailer instead wanted to increase awareness of the jewelry brand, ads could be served more frequently to customers who match the demographics and interests being targeted.

To ensure that your business is prepared for customers to take the actions you desire, you can create customer personas. A persona is a fictional customer whose characteristics match those of your target audience. It outlines details about your ideal customers that are related to their demographics and interests. The objective is to help you better understand why they make the decisions they choose so you can better influence their buying behavior.

Using the example of the online jewelry retailer, a customer persona may help the retailer determine that the target audience's annual income will be a factor that causes them not to purchase the high-end jewelry being advertised. Then, the retailer could use the details of their customer's income to advertise a more appropriate line of jewelry for that audience.

The indicators of your performance will be dependent on the audience you target and the objectives you set for your ad campaigns. Targeting customers whose demographics and interests are highly-relevant to what you sell will ensure the ad performance meets reasonable expectations.

Before beginning a social media advertising campaign, clearly define your objective. If the result you want to see is increased awareness of your brand, then measuring your ads' impressions will identify how many times the ad was seen by your target audience.

Objectives such as website traffic or online sales will require you to identify the rate of customers clicking your ads and the percentage of those customers who then make a purchase after landing on your site. The customer research you conduct and the personas you create can help drive great performance, but if the ads are not meeting your goals, you may need to revisit the data you have about your audience and clarify details that could be impacting your targeting methods.

Action Checklist

1. Research which social media platforms and content formats are generating the most interactions between brands and customers in your industry.

2. Increase exposure of your marketing messages by publishing them across multiple platforms and formats.

3. Schedule time to interact with customers and gather input on ways to enhance their experiences with your brand.

4. Analyze the growth potential of any enhancements to the customer experience by measuring the risks and alignment with your company's objectives.

5. Research the demographics and interests of your target audience and use those details to target ads to new customers.

6. Identify a specific action that you want customers to take when they see your ad and provide an experience that will support customers in taking that action.

Email Marketing

Email Content that Adds Value

Your email marketing can generate returning customers with value-based content that feeds a desire or solves a common problem within an industry. Value-based content connects customers' desires to the experience they will have with your brand. Writing this content will require you to research what your ideal customers truly value in the products or services you sell.

The objective is to learn first-hand from a meaningful group of customers rather than making an assumption based on your knowledge of the business or industry. No matter what your business sells, your email marketing content should demonstrate how your brand's offerings meet the specific needs of your customers and entice them to take an action that is valuable to your business such as redeem a coupon for use at your store.

Consumer-focused businesses may choose to write value-based content that connects customers' interests to the lifestyle of the brand. In these situations, your email marketing content can provide a profitable return if it, for example, introduces new products or services.

"Your email marketing content should demonstrate how your brand's offerings meet the specific needs of your customers."

In a business-to-businesses context, your content

may connect how your solutions can solve everyday problems faced by the readers or their customers. This content can acknowledge the problems that you discover during your research and then highlight your solutions, presenting your brand as the hero.

Once you have defined the value you will present in your email marketing content, you will need to consistently deliver your content. Email inboxes are a crowded space, so executing with excellence is a critical factor for high performance. One tool for this purpose is a content calendar with your past and upcoming email content, the mailing list, and the scheduled delivery dates and times.

By maintaining one reference point for content, you will be able to identify what content your customers have or have not already seen. Your customers are your biggest fans and they want to engage with your brand often. Content calendars make consistent email delivery very efficient. They can help you manage your email marketing schedule while you benefit from the resulting customer interactions.

There are three critical metrics to help you gauge the success of your email marketing. The first metric is your open rate, the percentage of customers opening your emails. Analyze your open rates across multiple campaigns to the same audience. The objective is to determine which combination of these details could lead to optimized campaigns in the future:

- Content in subject lines

- Days of week when emails were delivered
- Times of day when emails were delivered

You will need to correlate your highest and lowest open rates to the subject lines and delivery of your emails. Over time, you can test various subject lines to find words and phrases that are more likely to entice customers to open your emails.

You may also notice that your customers are more likely to open your emails on certain days of the week or at certain times. By analyzing which days and times result in the highest open rate, you can adjust your email delivery schedule and increase the open rates of your future emails.

The second email marketing metric to analyze is your click-through rate, which is the percentage of customers that open your email and click a link within it to visit your website. This metric is important when your site needs to support customers in taking other actions like reading a new blog post.

The most effective way to increase your click-through rate is by testing various calls to action. Your calls to action should entice customers to visit your website so they can perform a specific action. As you brainstorm what your call to action might say, keep it relevant to the action your customers will take once they land on your site. Some simple calls to action that will get you started include:

- Save 20% Now
- Try It for Free
- Get Started Today

The third email marketing metric to analyze is your conversion rate, which is the percentage of customers that clicked-through to your website and then took the specific action you intended for them to take. Your conversion rate can be affected by numerous factors including:

- the audiences targeted with the email
- how often the content on your site's landing page encourages customers to act
- ease for customers to act based on the landing page design and navigation

Marketing Your Email Newsletter

Your email marketing lists should contain current customers that have opted-in to receiving your newsletters. Buying a list is not going to generate the quality results you need for profitable email campaigns. Therefore, it's critical that you market your newsletter so you can continuously expand your database of newsletter subscribers who opted-in willingly.

Evaluate your owned media channels such as websites or social media for the visibility they could generate around your email program if used as marketing channels. There should be a volume of traffic that is significant in comparison to your brand's entire audience, plus high levels of engagement from the audiences on those channels.

Afterwards, determine how you can best approach the marketing of your newsletter within the available real estate of your online channels or within the schedules for your marketing communications.

"Your email marketing lists should contain current customers that have opted-in to receiving your newsletters."

When choosing marketing real estate on your website, for example, there's not much use to burying your marketing copy deep inside one webpage. Customers often enter websites through a variety of channels, and therefore, not all customers will see the same webpages. So, you will need to account for that behavior.

By placing your marketing message in your website's header or footer, you could reach all visitors with your marketing copy, no matter which webpages they browse. However, using those may not work for you, depending on the design of your site.

To help you decide where on your website that your marketing copy can reach the most customers, search for free web analytics tools. They can provide clear data about which pages customers use to enter your website. By uncovering which pages are the site's popular entry points, you can find available real estate to market your email newsletter.

Capture your customers' attention with imagery and catchy marketing copy that reflects your brand and stands out from the surroundings. Craft your marketing copy to include a strong call to action that draws attention and entices customers to click through to a landing page. On that page, you can encourage them to subscribe to your email program.

There are two advantages to creating a landing page where visitors can subscribe to your email program. The first is that you can lead customers directly to it from any other owned media channels to maximize visibility of your email program and increase subscriptions.

For example, brands with a strong social media following can send their audiences directly towards their website's subscription page. Otherwise, that brand would have waited much longer for that same audience of customers to eventually visit their website and maybe click through to the subscription page.

The second advantage of using a landing page for email program subscriptions is that you can write content that reflects the value of your newsletter and shows what other subscribers have received in the past such as special promotions. With content that sheds light on the value of your newsletters, you can increase the likelihood of converting many visitors into email program subscribers.

Encouraging Customer Opt-in

When customers arrive to your landing page, the content should present the value that real subscribers gain from your email newsletters. That value often includes early access to promotions or solutions to common industry problems.

Your objective with this content is to excite the audience about receiving that same value by subscribing to your newsletters. This content should favor quality over quantity because its objective is to engage customers enough that they subscribe.

Your subscription form should fulfill your needs for successful email campaigns and should also be short enough that customers don't abandon the form before completion. Aside from the obvious requirements such as name and email address, identify what other information could enhance the performance of your newsletters.

> "When customers arrive to your landing page, the content should present the value that real subscribers gain from your email newsletters."

If you sell to other businesses and you serve multiple markets, you may find a profitable return in emailing industry-specific newsletters. This would give you a valid reason to require a customer's industry when they subscribe.

If your company sells to consumers, you may find a

profitable return in segmenting your customers based on their interests. For example, a department store could enhance their email campaigns' success by grouping some customers into email lists related to designer clothing and other customers into email lists related to outdoor clothing.

To increase your subscriptions and optimize the marketing campaigns that generate landing page traffic, you must begin analyzing these three metrics. The first metric is the amount of views that your landing page received since you began marketing it. The objective behind measuring page views is not as simple as how many visits the page received. Your analysis of this metric should identify which owned media channels are driving the most traffic and the least traffic to your landing page.

That data can help you increase traffic by boosting your marketing efforts for the channels that are performing well. On the channels where your marketing is not driving much traffic, adjust your marketing campaign to encourage more customers to click through to your site's landing page.

The second metric to analyze is related to your email program's form submissions. Determine how many customers are beginning to fill out your subscription form, but then discarding it. The reasons for them discarding will vary, but one reason may be a complex interface. You can test new subscription form templates that ask less questions, ask the same questions in a simpler manner, or offer a drop-down menu for customers to choose their answers.

The third metric to analyze is the percentage of landing page views that resulted in a subscription. This is different than identifying how many customers submitted or discarded a form. This metric signals the health of your efforts and can help you find opportunities to increase your email program subscriptions.

By analyzing the percentage of landing page traffic that results in subscriptions, you can determine:

- how your landing page content and design can encourage subscriptions more often
- how many subscriptions you will receive if you increase page visits by 20 percent, for example

Action Checklist

1. Research what your ideal customers value in the products or services you sell.

2. Write value-based email content that connects your customers' interests and needs to the experiences they will have with your brand.

3. Evaluate your owned media channels to identify which could be valuable outlets as you market your email newsletter.

4. Drive newsletter subscriptions by leading customers towards a designated landing page.

5. Write landing page content that excites customers about the value they will gain from your newsletters.

6. Create short subscription forms while still gathering the customer details you need to target email campaigns at relevant audiences.

Website Content

Enhancing Visibility of Online Content

Websites are the most critical component to online visibility. Think of your website as the hub for your online branded content. It should be updated regularly with company news, industry involvement, and relevant marketing campaigns. Remember that your website is the first point of interaction between you and many of your customers. Don't reduce your site to just a showcase of your products or services.

> "Think of your website as the hub for your online branded content."

As mentioned earlier, a content calendar can help you think ahead about your marketing content. Schedule a variety of content such as press releases, sales promotions, or involvement with industry events. Also, add republished content to your calendar to extend visibility over time.

Content can be reused across all web-based platforms. Extend exposure of your marketing content by using your website to republish content from other outlets. For example, if your brand has a social media presence, you can embed the social media feed on your website to extend the reach of that content. If your company recently contributed to an industry blog, link to the blog from your site and designate space to provide context about your contribution.

As you strive to create a unified perception of your brand, the content you publish or republish to your website should include uniform brand messaging. This consistency across your content will allow your website to become a branded hub for your online ecosystem of content. In addition, as your customers journey from your other marketing outlets to your website, you will be building on the messages that differentiate your brand from the competition.

> "Extend exposure of your marketing content by using your website to republish content from other outlets."

To extend the reach of your marketing content through your website, you must analyze the impact of the content's visibility and discover which topics of content your customers are interacting with most.

By analyzing which content your customers interact with the most, you ensure that your limited website real estate is used for marketing content that engages customers. After gathering and analyzing the data, you will be able to present topics that your customers will respond to, ensuring your brand wins more of their attention, and consequently, their business.

Driving Sales with Web Experiences

You can provide an exceptional online experience for your customers if you take time to study how they navigate through your website to find content. Understanding your customers' navigation patterns can help you enhance your website interface and increase sales due to better findability of your products or services.

If you provide a clear path for customers to find what they want, they can make a buying decision rather than leaving your website for a competitor. To begin understanding the website struggles your customers experience and identify clearer paths to your content, gather a small focus group of your ideal customers to engage in a card-sorting exercise.

> "Increase sales due to better findability of your products or services."

Card sorting tests individuals on how they anticipate content to be structured on a website. It can help you understand where your customers expect to find specific content. This is important for website content because it helps you account for all navigational paths your customers may take to find content that leads to sales. Those insights will later help you design a navigational path that leads customers to the content they desire.

As an example, imagine a customer shopping for frozen pizza on a grocery website. If the site offered two paths to navigate, one named "Frozen Foods" and another named "Pizza," the customers could expect to find frozen pizza by following either link, even though one is more obvious than the other.

Card sorting may bring to light that visitors search for frozen pizza through both paths but do not find it with the "Frozen Foods" link. It would be profitable for the grocery site to make their frozen pizzas available through both paths.

The insights that you derive from such research can be valuable for websites focused on e-commerce, lead generation, or supporting a brand. You should first define a clear objective for changes made to your website such as growing sales, producing leads, or increasing consumption of marketing content. This will ensure that all enhancements are aligned with your vision for growing your business.

Ensuring Customer-centricity in Content

For your website content to engage customers, it must answer their questions or meet their needs in some way. This is known as customer-centric content, and it engages the audience by highlighting the value that customers receive from a specific product, service, or brand.

Customer-centric content should be prevalent across your website, and to achieve that, you can audit your content to ensure it meets the standards of you and your customers. Maintaining a spreadsheet of your content inventory can help you manage your new and existing content.

This spreadsheet should organize content details related to the target audience and content owners. The details you include should help you determine what content is aligned with your strategic plan(s) such as highlighting product value to customers and removing existing content that is not an aid in that effort.

> "Customer-centric content should be prevalent across your website."

When writing content that is aligned to a broader strategy, a spreadsheet of your content inventory can help by organizing many critical details related to findability, target audience, and content. Those details can help you align new and existing content with the objective of presenting customer-centric content.

The spreadsheet should organize each webpage within its own row, then be followed with columns of information related to the webpage's content, audience, traffic, and findability. Here are some specific details that could get your spreadsheet started:

- Target audience
- Keywords
- Content description, topic, owner
- Webpage URL
- Webpage analytics
- Dates of modifications

Due to the important details managed in these spreadsheets, they must be updated regularly to reflect the status of your content. Otherwise you will be unable to use it in decision making or as a reference when you write new content.

For example, some details in your spreadsheet may include keywords which would be useful for identifying the search terms already being targeted by your existing webpages. With that information, you can expand your marketing efforts to target different, but relevant keywords in your new content. Other details such as content descriptions and target audience can ensure you write differentiated, yet relevant content for your customers that expands upon what your site already presents.

When analyzing any data related to your website content, reference your content spreadsheet. You can use it to correlate quantitative data about webpage traffic to details about keywords, content, and target audiences.

Imagine that you have two webpages named Webpage A and Webpage B. If 75% of visitors to Webpage A were new visitors, but only 25% of visitors to Webpage B were new visitors, you could reference the content details in your spreadsheet to analyze and replicate the winning combination of targeting and content from Webpage A.

Action Checklist

1. Reuse your marketing content across multiple online outlets to extend the exposure of your messages.

2. Create a unified perception of your brand in the industry through consistent use of your brand messaging in marketing content across the web.

3. Close more sales by defining and improving how customers navigate your website for content about your products or services.

4. Improve how customers navigate your website by conducting a card sorting exercise to learn how customers interact with your website's navigation and content.

5. Write customer-centric content that engages customers by answering or solving their questions, needs, and desires.

6. Align your new and existing content to the critical details of your broader content strategy with a spreadsheet that manages your content inventory.

Digital Analytics

URL Tracking

You can use URL tracking to analyze the performance of your online marketing campaigns, and then analyze the data to fine-tune your efforts and increase website traffic.

Many companies that market through online platforms such as social media will lead their customers back to their website via a link. To determine which content is most effective at increasing website traffic, the links that lead customers to a website should have tagged, trackable URLs.

That is important because it captures data about the traffic generated from those platforms. It also continues capturing data every time those customers return, providing insights into the long-term value of your marketing efforts. This allows your business to make data-driven decisions, which lead to better use of online marketing platforms.

A tag on a URL is a simple snippet of code appended to it so you can track the website traffic your URL generates. These tags are quick and easy to create each time you post marketing content with a link to your website. But, for you to capture and view any data, you must have a web analytics tool set up on your site.

Here's an example of a URL with an appended tag:
www.example.org/?utm_campaign=nameofcampaign&utm_medium=socialmedia&utm_content=marketingcontent

By appending a tag to your URLs, you can capture multiple data points from customers who click through such as a marketing campaign's name, medium, source, and content. You can enhance your marketing performance by correlating those data points to results. Based on your objectives and investment in online marketing, you may want to:

- identify the amount of new visitors directed to your website from certain online sources

- optimize your investment of time and finances by identifying which variations of content and online sources generated the most traffic, sales, or leads

The URL tags follow your full web address and begin with a question mark. A parameter such as "utm_campaign=" must always precede your campaign's name.

The campaign's name is whatever you call each of your marketing campaigns that lead customers towards your website such as "utm_campaign=Flash Sale".

The campaign's medium refers to the medium you used to lead customers towards your website such as "utm_medium=Social Media".

The campaign's source signals where your URL resided when customers clicked it to visit your website such as "utm_source=Sponsored Ad".

The campaign's content briefly describes the marketing content that the URL resides amongst such as "utm_content=Sale Ending Soon".

"By appending a tag to your URLs, you can capture multiple data points from customers who click through."

Be sure to create a clear objective for yourself before you begin tagging URLs in your marketing content. Keep a focus on finding the marketing content and online sources that generated website traffic and the actions customers took after landing on your website.

On an e-commerce website, an objective may be to determine the contribution social media marketing had on your sales. In that situation, you would use data from such customers to determine the number of transactions and the value of those transactions after customers had followed your link on social media back to your website.

On a website built to support a brand, the objective may be to determine how many customers downloaded a white paper after reading a snippet of its text in an email newsletter. Whatever your objective may be, ensure that it ties content and its source to a valuable customer action on your website.

Tag Management

Tag management systems offer many data points to help you make data-driven decisions that optimize your website and online marketing performance.

Those data-driven decisions can help you can enhance interactions that customers have with your brand online.

In fact, website tagging provides many opportunities to capture data that web analytics tools do not. By identifying the data that's required to achieve your business objectives, you can begin monitoring, testing, and optimizing the most critical aspects of your website. Even common tags can fulfill many different business objectives. Some of these include page views, clicks, form submissions, and timers.

> "Enhance interactions that customers have with your brand online."

Capturing page views can help you visualize the volume of traffic that your webpages receive whether that volume is low or high. From there, you can work to determine the causes for those traffic volumes and how you can adjust. For example, an e-commerce website may have data that reflects a much higher volume of page views for one product compared to others.

One way to derive insights from that data would be to determine which online medium contributes most of that web traffic. Perhaps that medium was a search engine, in which case, you could identify any differences in the search marketing approach on that product's webpage compared to others and replicate it.

Tags that capture clicks on valuable website features can help you benchmark their usage for future optimization efforts. A company offering downloadable white papers can use a tag to track the number of clicks on a download button. Once the data has been compiled, the company may test new webpage designs that make the download button more prominent, resulting in more downloads.

Gathering data about online form submissions can help you determine how many customers are completing your forms due to ease of use or discarding it due to a complex interface. If your data was to signal that customers are discarding their forms, you could test new form templates until you find one that creates better results.

Another common, yet powerful tagging opportunity is to use timers. Timers allow you to measure how long customers spend completing actions like watching a video, which can help you identify performance issues and enhance the experience for customers.

"Make data-driven decisions that optimize your website and online marketing performance."

Convert More Website Visitors into Customers

A large percentage of the website traffic you receive will not convert into customers. Therefore, it's critical that you optimize your website to convert as much traffic into customers as possible.

Conversion rate optimization, or CRO, requires you to gather data about the sources of your website traffic, the webpages where those visitors are landing, and the actions that those webpages encourage visitors to take.

CRO can help you determine each online touchpoint's contribution to conversions. With that information, improvements can be made across those touchpoints to encourage more visitors to convert into customers.

> "CRO can help you determine each online touchpoint's contribution to conversions."

Optimizing your website to convert more website visitors will require you to first document the online touchpoints between your business and your visitors. This could include marketing outlets, landing pages, or sales-related pages like product details or services.

Also, you will need to determine the intent of your visitors as they interact with your brand at each of these touchpoints. To convert more website traffic into customers, you must create a create a connection between what your customers currently need and what your business can offer to help them decide.

As you drive traffic into your website from various online sources, you must consider the intent that your visitors had when they clicked through. For example, a person may visit your website after conducting a search with a broad search term, which could signal that they are performing research about a product or service.

By considering their intent, you can write webpage content that encourages visitors to move closer towards a buying decision. Based on your business objectives, you may choose to offer:

- discount codes or coupons
- downloadable white papers

Once you have a clear understanding of what your visitors desire when landing on your website, you should write content that moves them closer towards making a buying decision. The quickest way to ensure your content is converting site visitors into customers is to conduct A/B testing.

That is a simple initiative where you test and compare the results of two variations of content to identify which content converts the highest percentage of website visitors into customers. With A/B testing, you can receive results within days and start presenting visitors with content that converts.

Before beginning any optimization efforts however, it is critical that you determine the results you want to achieve. Some common goals include converting a higher percentage of website visitors or increasing the average order value from visitors to an eCommerce site.

For example, a website that converts 2% of its visitors into customers may generate $5,000 in revenue. If that same website conducted testing to optimize their conversion rate, they may determine that a different variation of content converts 5% of customers and generates $12,500.

Action Checklist

1. Use trackable URLs in marketing campaigns to gather performance data, which you can use to fine-tune your efforts and increase web traffic.

2. Determine the reasons for campaign success or failure by analyzing data of your campaigns' sources, mediums, and content.

3. Enhance the interactions customers have with your brand by monitoring, testing, and optimizing the critical aspects of your website.

4. Use website tags to understand and influence your customers' behavior related to page views, clicks, form submissions, and more.

5. Provide an experience for customers that is relevant to the intent they have when visiting your website from various online sources.

6. Test multiple variations of content on your webpages to determine which is most effective at moving customers towards a buying decision.

Made in the USA
Middletown, DE
04 July 2019